This book entails some exaggerated information for the purpose of entertainment.

From GED to College Degree

(How to better control your successes & blessings)

Introduction

Like me, if you were born in the inner city, your parents were minorities, household was unstable and both parents possessed an addictive gene, chances are that you are a victim of the crack era. This reality increases our chances of being less than and never achieving our true goals in life. This was the knowledge I was so less than privileged to be cursed with. As a young black boy, I was taught to be grateful for the little things and to believe that luck would only bring true success for me. These things were taught to me indirectly. The worst way that you could teach a black child! *Failure was earned and success was a blessing.*

The child that made it out of the hood was *blessed*. Scholarships, sports contracts, good jobs or careers were blessings. He or she must have had an angel over them. Luck was a word often said to describe certain achievements as well. How do we get considered for a "*blessing*"? How can we get a break. What keeps us last in line for luck. **Is it because the color of our skin, the way we dress, the language we speak, level of education, our addresses or just a curse. Everybody can't be cursed! Is a curse true? If it is, how does it select it's victims?**

Of course my parents told me that I could be anything I put my mind to. They did love me. I believe they did the best that they could. They showed me successful blacks who made it in sports, blacks who built homes, blacks who owned big businesses, black bankers, pastors and blacks who fought for our freedom. It wasn't that I didn't see any success for blacks, I just had a few questions. Why were we the minority of the successful world? The answers I got were limited. "Work hard and stay out of trouble and you can change it." Work hard on what? They also exposed me to doubt. Showing me the list of the presidents of the United States, exposing me to history and although we've made progress as a country, I felt we still had a long way to go. Even if I was blessed to make it, will I be alone? If I'm not alone and some of my brothas and sistas are there, will we still be the minority of the successful world?

Did I mention that my parent's relationship was strained as well? Drugs, alcohol and all the issues that come with it. Typical issues that people had from my neighborhood. Around this time, the foundation "Grandma's and Grandpa's values" were good, but crumbling because the values that they instilled in the families were being replaced by society's pleasures. Why was pleasure so important that the majority of their time was spent trying to achieve it? Our birthday parties were turned into adult parties after a certain time. We were told to either go to bed or go in our own rooms and watch TV. They would gamble playing Spades, drink, smoke Weed and eat Blue Claw Crabs.

How does this have anything to do with me getting a GED?

It doesn't, these factors can contribute to us starting bad habits and increase our chances of becoming addicted to drugs and alcohol, creating unwanted memories, making it difficult to have healthy social relationships and it could leave us without hope of achieving our true goals in life. This book is not only about hope and encouragement, but it entails the tools we will need to be better in control of our successes and blessings. Throughout this book, we will go over key factors of how we may have gotten to our current thought process and how we can change and or progress in any way we want. I will share my life experiences, we will reference back to previous events in my life and I will explain how our perceptions of current events can be shaped by past experiences. You'll also be educated on key points in our lives that we sometimes neglect. Paying attention to detail and studying ourselves can increase the possibility of us being the best people we can possibly be. Holistic Health is the goal and I believe we can achieve it by properly assessing ourselves using what clinicians call the **Biopsychosocial assessment** (George L. Engel, 1977). I know! "What the hell is that?". I got you! It's putting the facts (strengths & weaknesses) from your **Biological** makeup, **Psychological** makeup and **Social/Sociocultural** experiences on the table to assess ourselves properly in efforts to create plans to achieve our desired goals. The chapters will be somewhat out of the order from the way this model is spelled to give us a better understanding of how these aspects of our lives can have an effect on one another.

Chapter 1
Biological

"Playing the cards you're dealt." That phrase can be taken 1,000 different ways. Some people have to play this game of life with missing limbs, HIV, cancer, birth defects, heart problems, diabetes or a ton of other medical issues. Some people were born with illnesses and some developed them throughout their lives. Me, I was born with a brain tumor. My condition was not discovered until I was 9 years old. I remember it like it was yesterday. I kept complaining of headaches and my mother thought that I was just trying to get out of going to school. This particular day she let me stay home. It was snowing outside and the ground was covered with about a good 2 feet of snow. We were walking to the corner store and as we got to the steps of the store, I fell. She yelled at me, "get up." I could not feel my right side. I couldn't get up. She told me again, "get up." By that time she realized that it was something really wrong. The owner of the store called the Ambulance and they took me to the hospital. While at the hospital, my mom was told that her oldest child and only son had a brain tumor in the cerebellum region of his brain. That was not it. At this time, this condition was also rare and not many doctors had the experience with it. She was told that there had to be an emergency surgery and that I had a 50/50 chance of surviving it.

Although I made it out of surgery and the tumor was not cancerous, there was still a large demand on my family to make sure that I rehabilitated from the hospitalization. My vocal cords, arms and legs were weakened from me being sedated and in the hospital bed for months. The doctor told me that although I will eventually be walking and talking normally soon, I cannot be allowed to play contact sports because they placed a Shunt in my head to drain the excess fluid from my brain. He told me that the Shunt had a cord that traveled down my chest, past my stomach and to my private area so I can urinate the fluid out and that the cord would grow with me as I become an adult. My neck muscles had got used to me being in the bed with a tilt, so when I was released from the hospital I walked with a tilted neck. Throughout my life I've had to deal with restrictions caused by my condition. I had to visit the doctors more regularly than someone who wasn't in my position. My family's structure had to be adjusted due to me having physical restraints.

I grew to love contact sports, but I was told I couldn't play any because of my condition. Having medical issues set me apart from others who were "normal" so I thought. Although I was smart and knew the latest news in sports along with the lyrics to the most popular songs, I still was limited to what I could do and how social I could be. There were games that we played in the inner city called hard to the body (punching each other in the body until someone gives up), killer man (throwing the football up and gang tackling who ever caught it) and rough house (every man for himself on the basketball court). These games entailed hard contact and often left it's players bleeding, knocked out cold and with broken bones. I was not allowed to play these games because I could possibly be hurt far worse than others. The fact that I had these limitations eventually led me to be teased and outcasted. To me, this sure didn't feel like a ***blessing***…. "If it wasn't, was it an ***earned failure or a curse***?" I was confused………

Let's talk!

Let's just leave my issues aside right now and think about any medical issue someone may have. If you're born with an illness, it requires regular maintenance to keep the ill person healthy (mentally and physically). Living in poverty, not being educated properly on gaining and maintaining health and without quality medical attention available can increase the chances of someone becoming ill or not receiving the proper care it takes to maintenance one's quality of life if they were born ill. This shit is no joke. Tons of other things can be affected along the way.

Living with a medical issue is difficult. Just being different and limited in what you can do is hard. Especially on a child. The everyday stress of having to abide by a schedule and or series of ritual procedures to keep yourself healthy is not the life you would ask for. So it's not difficult to understand how not just the illness, but the stress that comes with it can affect someone's life in ways they do and do not even recognize. The person, family and society have to assume roles to compensate for the person with the illness and this could cause issues within itself.

Chapter 2

Social/Sociocultural experiences

We learn many values and form perspectives from our upbringing in the home in combination with our experiences in the world outside of our homes (directly or indirectly). These values can complement one another or one can totally conflict with the other. Some know when to use home or street knowledge to identify or deal with an issue. I remember playing in the park at 8 years old with friends and us seeing; empty valves, empty small manilla envelopes, plastic bags, aluminum foil, broken car antennas, glass pipes, used needles, cigarette wrap packs and cigarette butts. The wild thing is, we knew exactly what they were and what they were used for. These things were drug paraphernalia. We could even spot the very people who used, sold drugs or did both. Drug dealing and using was "normal" in my neighborhood so we knew who was who. The other things that were considered "normal" were; robberies, assaults, murders, incarcerated loved ones, poverty, no parental supervision and missing fathers. Because we lived in the hood, my mother prepared me by letting me know who was who and what was what. She told me what to stay away from and what to look out for. I was sent to my grandmother's house on the weekends and she made us go to church every Sunday. But after church, it was back to reality. The hood! I didn't feel like the lessons taught at church or values taught at home could help me deal with my reality. It just never applied to me...... The pastor was not me and my mother wasn't me...... It was a new day and even if they grew up in this environment, it definitely was not at this time........ They didn't understand, and now that I look at it, neither did I........ It was hard when you were knee deep in it....

The things I thought were odd was odd. At 12 years old, I went to my first party in the neighborhood. My mother thought I was at my friend's house. I was with some older friends in the neighborhood and one of them was the DJ of this party. He ran out of music and asked me to go around the corner to get him some more records. As I was crossing the street, gunshots started to go off. I looked to my right and a man was being shot repeatedly about 50 feet away from me. I remember standing there and watching the bullets go through his body. Wow, he was standing there and taking shot after shot without falling. Then I realized, bullets can be seen at night going through the air. I thought it was entertaining. The thought that a bullet could have mistakenly hit me never crossed my mind. This was regular everyday shit to me. When I got back to the party, all I could talk about was that I seen the sparks from the bullets fly past me. The fact that a crime was being committed or a life could have been taken was never mentioned and at that time, I didn't feel like it should've been. It was like I was programed to see this shit as nothing but everyday life and normal. After a little, if something similar didn't go on for a while, I thought that was odd…….

We had little respect for others. Pimps, prostitutes, drug dealers, drug users and alcoholics were regularly sighted performing their everyday duties. We found the Pimps to be funny. They were drug users as well. They would roam the streets, chase prostitutes and beat them if they didn't make the expected amount of money for the day. This shit was funny to us as kids…… Pimps would call the prostitutes "Bitches." I used to hear stories about pimps having money and being flashy, but not in my hood. Pimps were broke as hell! We later found out that some pimps fathered the children that their prostitutes had…. Weird, but normal in my hood. The Pimps and their so called Bitches were some of our friends, family members and parents. The Pimps would tell us, "hey, y'all get off the street and go to school!" We would say, "take your own fucking advice." We used to think, "how the hell can a drug using piece of shit low life Pimp tell us to do some shit he can't do?' We never respected them. In fact, we use to throw rocks at them and run. Them dudes couldn't catch us.

The drug dealers had the money and we looked up to them. We saw their success as achievable. I remember seeing them pull up in the hood with Monte Carlos and Toyota .8's with loud speaker systems and pictures painted on the hoods. They used to wear the big gold rope chains with the bracelets to match….. and…. oh yeah… the 4 finger rings! They didn't respect the Pimps and Bitches neither. Guess that's why we didn't. We knew they were doing wrong because of what was taught to us, but we seen them do more good than bad. They would buy clothes, sneakers, coats, school supplies and even food for those who needed the help. They seemed to be the saviours even though they sold drugs to our families. Shit, they were just selling….. We didn't feel like they forced them to buy the shit. And although the drug dealers seemed to be different, they said the same things the Pimps said, "hey, y'all get off the street and go to school!" We used to say, "Why? We don't need school to get money like you."

We just felt like our fate was written and we'll go out like anybody else (dealers, pimps, prostitutes and store owners). The alcoholics would be in front of the liquor stores early in the morning. They would look and smell like they didn't wash for days. Now that I think about it, that might've been the truth….. They didn't wash...... I remember them asking us for change to get them a drink........ I would think, "we're kids, you that fucked up that you'll ask kids for money so you can get a drink?" We would tell them, "fuck you, get a job," then we'd throw rocks at them and run..... The liquor store owners would come out periodically and yell at us, "hey, y'all get off the street and go to school!!" Every now and then we'll hear of one of the store owners getting robbed and killed or the drug dealers getting arrested for murder or possession of drugs. The drug dealers would even get robbed and killed themselves. We would also hear of the pimps and prostitutes getting arrested, murdered or even overdosing on drugs. This became normal to us. We would expect it after a while.

Hearing about people getting locked up, people dying from being shot, stabbed, beat to death or overdosing on drugs was damn near everyday life for us. It was just something to talk about after a while. But nothing prepared me for the murder of my best friend Star. We would take turns rapping on the corner and my boy was pretty good. Star was his rap name. Star and I were inseparable. It was about 10 to 15 of us who really hung out and we all were pretty tight, but Star was the one I hung with the most. I remember us always having conversations of getting the hell out of the ghetto and never coming back. We would talk about how it was odd that we messed up our own communities, but left everyone else's clean. I remember us taking the N.J. Transit bus and riding it just to see other places. We never planned to go anywhere in particular. We would look out the window of the bus as we ride through the suburbs and claim things like cars, woman and houses. We even looked at the people coming out of the stores wearing suits and we would say, "I'm gonna dress like that too....." See, Star and I shared something special, a dream. Our dream was real and we saw it. **For some crazy reason, we felt like we could earn it.** He seemed to be the only one that understood me too. We would talk from sun up to sun down about our dream and we promised each other that one day we'll make it a reality, not only for us, but for everyone that looked like us too. I never knew that one day I would have the responsibility of carrying out our dream by myself.

I felt my life would never be the same after he passed. Prior to his passing, I had landed my first job cleaning the showroom floor of a neighborhood car lot and they called me into work this day. Star and the rest of the fellas were going to the park to workout. I wanted to go, but I just got the job so I told the fellas I'll catch up with them later. After getting off work, I came home, ate and went right to sleep. When I woke up the next morning, I realized I never spoke to my boy Star. I was running late to work that morning so I had to rush in. While working, I got a call from a close friend that I called my sister (Nef). When I picked up the phone, Nef said, " hey bro....... I heard the news..... are you ok?" I paused and thought for a second. Usually when we talk about news, we get right to it, but when the shit is that close to home, we make broad statements like the one she made, "I heard the news.....," followed by, are you ok?" so I hung the phone up. Minutes later my mother pulled up to the car lot and she said, "get in the car......

I had to be the one to tell you, it's Star.........." I immediately fell to the ground and thought, "No more dream!!! It was done!! Fuck life!! This shit ain't fair!!" My life was never the same after that moment. I felt like my life was *cursed* and I was forever a *failure*! It seemed like my feelings would be this way for the rest of my life.....

Let's Talk

We all have our own experiences. Some have worse experiences than others. Getting shot, stabbed, kidnapped, robbed and raped are a few. Some people have been abandoned as children by their parents, some people wished they were abandoned by them and maybe their upbringing would've been better. How about the people who were abused (physically & emotionally) throughout their childhood. No, what about the ones who were molested over and over by family members or the ones who were sold for drugs and the same shit happened to them. What about not having the necessities. How about being the kid who had to wear hand-me -downs or clothes from the church that led them to be picked on by the neighborhood kids because their family couldn't afford to buy the latest style clothes. There's tons of other situations I can mention, but you get the picture. This can lead to problems far more intense than we can handle on our own.

Chapter 3
Psychological

Crazy….. Although we are getting better with our understanding of mental illness, sometimes our cultural beliefs and myths of what we see or feel may get in the way. "You just trippen." Bipolar Disorder, Schizophrenia and a host of other disorders are real. There are other disorders that we could develop throughout life such as; Post Traumatic Stress Disorder, Major Depressive Disorder, Substance Use Disorder and many more. These disorders can be brought on by exposure to traumatic events and or substance consumption in conjunction with own genetic makeup. We were told some people had demons in them.

I remember seeing homeless people walking down the street, talking to themselves and sometimes dancing real hard to some music that wasn't even there. As kids we would laugh, but as an adult, I would wonder. "I wonder if he/she could be helped? Did that happen over night or did they get slipped some bad drugs?" I remember seeing people get extra paranoid after they've been robbed or even shot too. Family members of love ones who'd passed from the results of having chronic illnesses, natural causes or being murdered would act differently. It was like they had less motivation to live anymore. Those were the people I understood the most. To me, there was nothing crazy about that.

I recall feeling lonely after Star passed. Even if I was with my other friends or family, I still felt by myself. I would sit on Star's step in the mornings for no reason, just thinking. The thing is, I don't even remember what I was thinking about. Just sitting there. I did it consistently for months too. When I sensed I was enjoying life a little,

I quickly sabotaged my happiness by discontinuing the very activity I was enjoying. By this time, I distanced myself from my family and other friends. It seemed like the only mood I could control was the one I had when I **failed** or felt **failed** by society. Having the need to be in control of my feelings, I often *earned failure* to feel normal. I didn't feel like I was in line for a *blessing*. I dropped out of school because I felt the dream was gone! No more hope……….. I later found out I was severely depressed.

Let's talk

Most of us ain't trying to hear that…. We'll at least where I'm from they're not… Culturally we say, "man up!" Many of us suppress our true feelings just to conform to the everyday culture of our homes or neighborhoods. Is that the case? Do you have things you're holding on to?

Obtaining or/and maintaining mental health is important. If you feel like you have suppressed feelings, any uncontrollable mood swings, you get alarmed easily when being alarmed is not typically warranted or you have any uncontrollable urges to seek substances (drugs and alcohol) or events (sex, gamling, criminal acts, eating, etc.), don't hesitate to ask for help! Even though some cases require professional help, not all need to be treated in that manner. Some can be treated by getting away from the "norm" or treating yourself to your favorite food or activity periodically. Even having conversation with a non bias friend would help. Being mentally healthy is important!

Assessment results

I never knew how my biological makeup, psychological makeup and social/sociocultural experiences affected my decision making and ultimately my fate as a black man in this world. Hell, I didn't know these things existed. I felt like my life was already written and I had no sayso in the matter. *It was what it was.*

It felt like my dream was lost when Star passed because he was the only one that would totally except me for who I was. Looking back at my life, I was depressed way before he died. I thought the dream died when Star died because I wasn't confident enough in myself to carry it out on my own after he passed. The truth is, I wasn't confident enough while he was here. I felt I would be just another statistic because I was disabled, born in the hood and pretty much raised by the streets. Going to school and staying out of the streets like the neighborhood drug dealers, users and store owners said looked like a waste of time. It was a small percentage that made it out of the hood and did something with themselves. I really didn't feel in control of my life until I learnt this process. *My therapist taught me the biopsychosocial assessment..... He told me that I was intelligent enough to go through this process on my own and if I did it right, I would increase the possibility of being in control of my successes and blessings.*

"My therapist was right….. I have successfully completed and self published my first book!"

Purpose

This book and mission is the dream Star and I had! Please join us! The title was inspired by my latest achievement (GED) and my now journey (to earn a College Degree). Using this process (biopsychosocial assessment) has helped me get here and I know it will help me go to the top if I continue to use it effectively. You can do it too. ***Let's grow together!***

How to better control your successes & blessings

You are unique and so is the **blessing** that you have already been given. There is not 1 person on this earth like you. **Your success is defined by your ability to be better than what you were yesterday.** When you made the decision to change and acted on your thought, you were already **successful**. To maintain your **success** takes consistent work. Following this process will help you.

The process of your self assessment (biopsychosocial assessment)

First set your goal. Then start assessing yourself, but only pay attention to aspects of your life (biological, psychological and social/sociocultural experiences) that would assist in or hurt your chances of achieving your set goal. Be mindful to take your time with this process to ensure you don't miss anything important. Don't hesitate to get professional (licensed) assistance with this process if you feel it is necessary.

- Look at your biological makeup. Are you tall or short? Are you physically strong or weak? Are you healthy or unhealthy? Are you overweight? Do you have any chronic illness? If so, have you been or are you currently receiving the attention your illness requires? Do you have any chronic illnesses that run in your family? Look at these things and measure your strengths along with weaknesses. Write them down!

- Look at your psychological makeup. Have you ever been diagnosed and treated for any mental health issues in the past? If so, are you currently stable? Are you mostly happy or sad? Do you have any unresolved/unaddressed issues such as;

26

grief over the death of a love one/s or any unresolved/unaddressed experiences such as rape, molestation, abuse, trauma, etc. Look at these things and measure your strengths along with weaknesses. Write them down!

- Look at your social/sociocultural experiences. Who raised you? Where did you grow up? Who were your friends? How was it growing up? How were your experiences perceived then and how are they perceived now? Who do you socialize with now? Look at these things and measure your strengths along with weaknesses. Write them down.

These questions are just a guideline. I am pretty sure you can come up with more to ask yourself in these areas to get better results. If you feel comfortable, ask someone you trust to help you answer these questions about yourself to get another perspective of what your strengths and weaknesses may be in these areas.

Embrace your strengths and address your weaknesses. After identifying your strengths, let them work for you in the pursuit of your goal. Make them stronger by exercising them (If it's knowledge, learn more. If it's muscle, lift more weights). After identifying your weaknesses, give them the necessary attention. Make sure your weaknesses are taken care of so that they don't hinder your process of success. If your identified weaknesses can be strengthened, by all means strengthen them. When you complete the biopsychosocial assessment on yourself and you begin the process of working on your identified strengths and weaknesses, it is then time to go from GED to College Degree.

Please continue.................

Start planning to earn your blessing today!

This book belongs to _____

Goal is_____

You will be closer to your goal than you have ever been in the next 30 days if you follow your own plans. This is day 1. The next 29 pages will be templates for daily activity towards your goal/s. You will put small tasks on your checklist. As you complete your tasks, you'll check them off (don't check it off if you didn't complete it). At the bottom of every checklist, there is a spot to journal. The journal area will be key to assess your progress. Write your feelings about the day's activities whether you're satisfied or not. By day 30, you'll be closer to your goal. That's if you haven't achieved it already by then!

Have fun earning your blessing!

Day #2

❑ _____

❑ _____

❑ _____

❑ _____

❑ _____

Daily journal

_____
_____
_____
_____
_____
_____
_____
_____
_____
_____
_____

The most unselfish thing you can do is be selfish....... (Herb Parsi)

"Nobody can benefit from you if you are not taken care of"

Day #3

❏ _____

❏ _____

❏ _____

❏ _____

❏ _____

Daily journal

_____
_____
_____
_____
_____
_____
_____
_____
_____
_____
_____
_____
_____

Focus!

Day #4

❏ _____

❏ _____

❏ _____

❏ _____

❏ _____

Daily journal

_____
_____
_____
_____
_____
_____
_____
_____
_____
_____
_____
_____

Make sure you're journaling……..

Day #5

❑ _____

❑ _____

❑ _____

❑ _____

❑ _____

Daily journal

_____
_____
_____
_____
_____
_____
_____
_____
_____
_____
_____
_____

Meet your challenges head on…………..

Day #6

❑ _____

❑ _____

❑ _____

❑ _____

❑ _____

Daily journal

_____

_____

_____

_____

_____

_____

_____

_____

_____

_____

_____

You got this………...

Day #7

❑ _____

❑ _____

❑ _____

❑ _____

❑ _____

Daily journal

_____
_____
_____
_____
_____
_____
_____
_____
_____
_____
_____
_____
_____

1 week down! Good job!

Day #8

❏ _____

❏ _____

❏ _____

❏ _____

❏ _____

Daily journal

_____
_____
_____
_____
_____
_____
_____
_____
_____
_____
_____

You are unique...... There is no one like you on this earth........

Day #9

❑ _____

❑ _____

❑ _____

❑ _____

❑ _____

Daily journal

_____
_____
_____
_____
_____
_____
_____
_____
_____
_____
_____
_____

If you stop now, you'll be depriving the world of what you got to offer!

Day #10

❑ _____

❑ _____

❑ _____

❑ _____

❑ _____

Daily journal

_____
_____
_____
_____
_____
_____
_____
_____
_____
_____
_____
_____

Consistency is the key!

Day #11

❏ _____

❏ _____

❏ _____

❏ _____

❏ _____

Daily journal

_____
_____
_____
_____
_____
_____
_____
_____
_____
_____
_____
_____

You are in control of your success!

Day #12

❑ _____

❑ _____

❑ _____

❑ _____

❑ _____

Daily journal

_____
_____
_____
_____
_____
_____
_____
_____
_____
_____
_____

Be great!

Day #13

❑ _____

❑ _____

❑ _____

❑ _____

❑ _____

Daily journal

_____
_____
_____
_____
_____
_____
_____
_____
_____
_____
_____
_____
_____

You can change the world...............

Day #14

❑ _____

❑ _____

❑ _____

❑ _____

❑ _____

Daily journal

_____
_____
_____
_____
_____
_____
_____
_____
_____
_____
_____

Week 2 is down.......... But who's counting?.................

Day #15

❑ _____

❑ _____

❑ _____

❑ _____

❑ _____

Daily journal

_____
_____
_____
_____
_____
_____
_____
_____
_____
_____
_____
_____
_____

Go!

Day #16

❏ _____

❏ _____

❏ _____

❏ _____

❏ _____

Daily journal

_____
_____
_____
_____
_____
_____
_____
_____
_____
_____
_____
_____

Prove this to yourself................

Day #17

❑ _____

❑ _____

❑ _____

❑ _____

❑ _____

Daily journal

_____
_____
_____
_____
_____
_____
_____
_____
_____
_____
_____
_____

Earn your blessing.............

Day #18

❑ _____

❑ _____

❑ _____

❑ _____

❑ _____

Daily journal

_____
_____
_____
_____
_____
_____
_____
_____
_____
_____
_____

Take what's yours………….

Day #19

❑ _____

❑ _____

❑ _____

❑ _____

❑ _____

Daily journal

_____
_____
_____
_____
_____
_____
_____
_____
_____
_____
_____
_____

Set a standard for others to follow.............

Day #20

❑ _____

❑ _____

❑ _____

❑ _____

❑ _____

Daily journal

_____
_____
_____
_____
_____
_____
_____
_____
_____
_____
_____

This is time to build your legacy…………..

Day #21

❑ _____

❑ _____

❑ _____

❑ _____

❑ _____

Daily journal

_____
_____
_____
_____
_____
_____
_____
_____
_____
_____
_____
_____

There is no one that can stop you now but you...............

Day #22

❑ _____

❑ _____

❑ _____

❑ _____

❑ _____

Daily journal

_____

_____

_____

_____

_____

_____

_____

_____

_____

_____

Don't give up on yourself.............

Day #23

❏ _____

❏ _____

❏ _____

❏ _____

❏ _____

Daily journal

_____
_____
_____
_____
_____
_____
_____
_____
_____
_____
_____
_____

Your blessing will come when it's time, just keep pushing!

Day #24

❑ _____

❑ _____

❑ _____

❑ _____

❑ _____

Daily journal

_____

_____

_____

_____

_____

_____

_____

_____

_____

_____

_____

Be resilient…………..

Day #25

❏ _____

❏ _____

❏ _____

❏ _____

❏ _____

Daily journal

_____
_____
_____
_____
_____
_____
_____
_____
_____
_____
_____
_____

Your vision is your vision……….. Don't expect them to see it right now!

Day #26

❑ _____

❑ _____

❑ _____

❑ _____

❑ _____

Daily journal

_____
_____
_____
_____
_____
_____
_____
_____
_____
_____
_____
_____

When your day comes, they will have no choice but to cheer!

Day #27

❑ _____

❑ _____

❑ _____

❑ _____

❑ _____

Daily journal

_____

_____

_____

_____

_____

_____

_____

_____

_____

_____

_____

Keep it going………….. Push!

Day #28

❑ _____

❑ _____

❑ _____

❑ _____

❑ _____

Daily journal

_____
_____
_____
_____
_____
_____
_____
_____
_____
_____
_____

You're almost there!

Day #29

❑ _____

❑ _____

❑ _____

❑ _____

❑ _____

Daily journal

_____

_____

_____

_____

_____

_____

_____

_____

_____

_____

_____

Keep your strength!

Day #30

❏ _____

❏ _____

❏ _____

❏ _____

❏ _____

Daily journal

_____

_____

_____

_____

_____

_____

_____

_____

_____

_____

Congratulation! You have been blessed all along...............

Keep earning your blessings and don't let no one else tell you it's not possible!

Made in the USA
Middletown, DE
07 January 2019